FUN WITH WORDS

SPELLING • STARTING WITH WORDS • FINDING FACTS • MAKING CHARTS

QEB Publishing

Editor: Amanda Askew
Design: Red Paper Design
Illustrator: Becky Blake

Educational consultants:
David and Penny Glover

First published in the UK in 2010 by
QED Publishing
A Quarto Group Company
226 City Road
London EC1V 2TT

www.qed-publishing.co.uk

A catalogue record for this book is
available from the British Library.

ISBN 978 1 59566 767 0

Printed in China

CONTENTS

ICT Notes for Parents

This book is helpful for supporting children both at home and in school. In the classroom, it can be tied in with work on English, science, and math.

Starting with Words: pages 36–63

THESE PAGES CAN BE USED TO SUPPORT COMPUTER CLASSES, OR CAN BE TIED IN TO HELP CHILDREN PRESENT HOMEWORK FOR ENGLISH, HISTORY, SOCIAL STUDIES, OR SCIENCE. THEY CAN BE ACHIEVED BY ENCOURAGING YOUR CHILDREN TO COLLECT AND DISCUSS ALL KINDS OF PRINTED INFORMATION, SUCH AS NEWSPAPERS, SIGNS, LABELS, MENUS, AND ADVERTISEMENTS. HELP YOUR CHILDREN TO IDENTIFY THE PURPOSE AND INTENDED AUDIENCE OF THE MATERIALS THEY FIND AND DISCUSS THE MESSAGE THEY THINK THE INFORMATION IS TRYING TO COMMUNICATE. ASK WHETHER THE PRESENTATION IS SUITABLE, AND IF THE MESSAGE GETS ACROSS.

ENCOURAGE YOUR CHILDREN TO REVIEW, EVALUATE, AND IMPROVE THEIR OWN WORK AT ALL STAGES. IF POSSIBLE, SHOW THEM WORK BY OLDER CHILDREN AND HELP THEM SEE HOW THIS WORK FULFILLS THE SAME GOALS THEY HAVE IN THEIR OWN WORK.

Finding Facts: pages 64–91

THESE PAGES CAN BE USED TO SUPPORT COMPUTER CLASSES, OR THEY CAN BE TIED IN TO CLASS- OR HOMEWORK IN ANY OTHER AREA OF THE CURRICULUM IN WHICH THE CHILDREN USE THE COMPUTER OR BOOKS TO RESEARCH A TOPIC AND RESEARCH INFORMATION.

PROVIDE SUITABLE TALKING BOOKS, AND BOOKS OR ENCYCLOPEDIAS ON CD-ROM FOR CHILDREN TO WORK WITH. MAKE SURE THE LANGUAGE IS APPROPRIATE FOR THEIR AGE AND THAT THERE ARE CLEAR CONTENTS, NAVIGATION AIDS, AND SEARCH FACILITIES THAT CHILDREN

WILL BE ABLE TO USE. GIVE CHILDREN PRECISE INSTRUCTIONS
SO THAT THEY RESEARCH TOPICS THAT HAVE LINKS TO
OTHER USEFUL, RELATED MATERIAL. HELP THEM TO IDENTIFY
AND TRY OUT DIFFERENT KEYWORDS, AND DISCUSS THE RESULTS OF THEIR SEARCHES.

ENCOURAGE CHILDREN TO WORK TOGETHER AND DISCUSS HOW TO FIND INFORMATION
USING A COMBINATION OF CONTENTS OR INDEX, FOLLOWING LINKS AND USING SEARCH
TERMS. HELP THEM TO TALK ABOUT WHICH KEYWORDS WERE MOST SUCCESSFUL AND WHY.
CHILDREN SHOULD BE ENCOURAGED TO REVIEW, EVALUATE, AND IMPROVE THEIR WORK AT
ALL STAGES.

Making Charts: pages 92–119

MAKE SURE THE PICTOGRAM COMPUTER SOFTWARE IS SET UP FOR THE CHILDREN TO USE.
THEY WILL NEED SUITABLE ICONS AVAILABLE. YOU WILL NEED TO CHOOSE SUITABLE TEXT
FONTS AND SIZES FOR THEM.

ENCOURAGE CHILDREN TO WORK TOGETHER AND DISCUSS OPTIONS AS THEY COLLECT
INFORMATION AND MAKE THEIR PICTOGRAMS. ASK THEM TO DISCUSS WHAT THEY ARE TRYING
TO FIND OUT. THIS WILL MAKE IT POSSIBLE TO ASSESS HOW SUCCESSFUL THEY ARE. REVIEW
THEIR FINISHED WORK AND ASK THEM TO TALK ABOUT WHY THEY CHOSE THE OPTIONS THEY
DID, AND WHY THEY REJECTED OTHERS. ASK THEM IF THEY CAN THINK OF ANY WAYS OF
IMPROVING THEIR WORK.

CHILDREN SHOULD BE ENCOURAGED TO REVIEW, EVALUATE, AND IMPROVE THEIR OWN WORK
AT ALL STAGES. IF POSSIBLE, SHOW THEM WORK BY OLDER CHILDREN AND HELP THEM TO SEE
HOW THIS FULFILS THE SAME GOALS THAT THEY HAVE IN THEIR OWN WORK.

NOTES FOR PARENTS AND TEACHERS

- Children learn new words daily, but they must use the words in order to remember them. Talk with your child using many different words as often as possible.

- Ask, "Do you know what this means?" when your child finds an unfamiliar word.

- Play word-based board games as well as party games such as charades.

- Read aloud to your children, even as they grow older.

- Encourage reading of any kind, whether it's a magazine, book or menu.

- Talk about what you are reading.

- Let your child use a bookmark or index card to cover sentences below the one that your child is reading.

- When possible, let children highlight material that they read. Colors can flag unfamiliar words, main ideas, or important information. If marking the text is not possible, use small adhesive notes or flags.

- After reading, take a few minutes to talk about these pages and summarize the materials. This will help your child remember what they have read and provide time to clarify understanding.

VOCABULARY AND COMPREHENSION

MONTHS OF THE YEAR

Read each question and point to the correct answer on the right.

1. Which month comes after February?

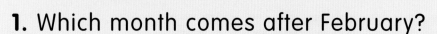

2. Which month comes before July?

3. Which month has three letters in its name?

4. Which month has six letters in its name?

5. Which is the first month of the year?

6. Which is the last month of the year?

January

February

March

April

May

June

July

August

September

October

November

December

PARTS OF THE BODY

Every part of your body has a name.
You have eyes, a nose, mouth and ears—
and that's just on your face.

Read each word and point to the correct part of the body.

knee

nose

neck

mouth

eye

head

leg

hand

arm

foot

ANIMALS

Every animal has a name, such as lion or dog.

Read each word and then point to the animals which belong in that group.

 **Farm animals**

cat

cow

lion

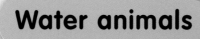 **Water animals**

pig

whale

shark

bear

 **Wild animals**

fish

hamster

zebra

 **Pets**

chicken

dog

A classroom is full of things. These things all have a name so you know what they are.

Look at each picture and point to the correct naming word.

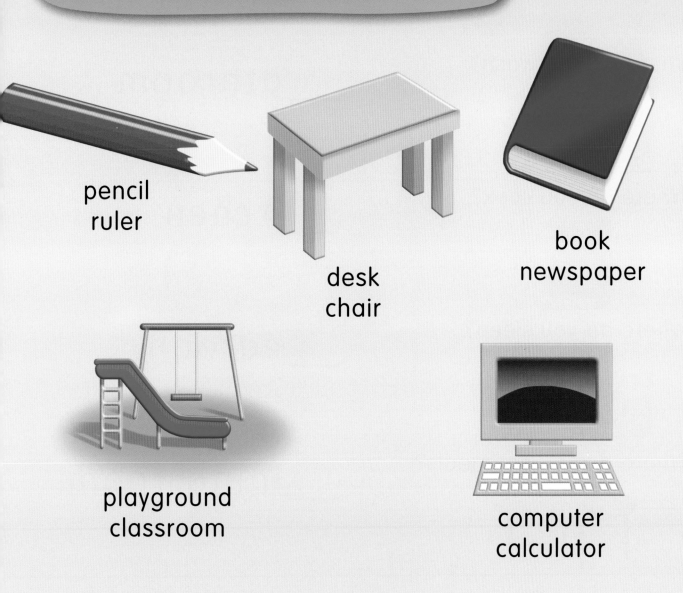

pencil
ruler

desk
chair

book
newspaper

playground
classroom

computer
calculator

AROUND THE **HOME**

You have many things around your home.
Each room and all the things in it have names.

Read each question, then point to the correct letter in the letter bank to complete the asnwer.

Letter bank

d   b   b   k

1. Where do you wash?

__athroom

2. Where do you cook?

__itchen

3. Where do you sleep?

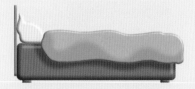

__edroom

4. Where do you eat meals?

__ining room

FEELINGS

You have many different feelings. Sometimes you are happy and sometimes you are sad.

Read each word, then point to the picture that you think matches.

angry

happy

scared

shy

confused

NOTES FOR PARENTS AND TEACHERS

- When you read with children, look for the parts of speech that they are learning. It exposes children to a variety of words and show how they are used.

- Let children see you write. Show them how you use writing tools, such as a dictionary, thesaurus and even electronic spell-check. Children should understand that writing is something that they might do in many situations.

- Help children create their own dictionary of words they want to remember. They can add to it any time. The dictionary can serve as a reference for spelling and parts of speech.

- Give children many opportunities to read the type of writing they will be doing. If children will be writing instructions, give them many kinds of instructions to look at, such as instructions for assembling a toy, a recipe or instructions for using a camera.

- Children should look for ways that the writer describes steps so that they are undetstandable.

- Do not write for children. This sends the message that it is hard!

- Give children checklists for proofing and revising. This sets goals as they reread their work and gives them something specifc to look for.

- Do not change the words you use because you are speaking to children. They will build their reading and writing vocabulary by hearing and using a variety of words.

- Give children special writing tools, such as pretty pencils, decorated paper and a thesaurus of their own.

- Look for things to praise in children's writing. Be specific, such as, "This sentence really tells me how exciting the trip was." This will help to build confidence, and reinforce the things that children are doing right.

NOUNS

Nouns are a person, a place, or a thing. A singular noun is one thing. A plural noun is many things.

Read the sentences. First point to the nouns that are people, then to the nouns that are places, and then to the nouns that are things.

Jenny stops at the A&M Grocery Store on her way home from school. Mrs. Ritter said to buy butter and some milk. They are going to make cookies! They will bring the cookies to Rosary Hill Nursery Home. That's where Jenny's grandma lives.

VERBS

Verbs are action words. The tense of a verb tells you when the action happens.

Verbs in the present tense are taking place now. Verbs is in the past tense have already happened.

Present   Peter walks the dog.
Past   Claire walked to school.

Present   Darren stops talking.
Past   Julia stopped running.

Present   Andrew sits on the floor.
Past   Susan sat on a chair.

Present   Dad tells Joe a story.
Past   Mr. Johnson told the
                class to be quiet.

ADJECTIVES

Adjectives are words that describe nouns. They tell you what kind of noun and how many.

Adjectives can also compare nouns. Some end in -er, or -est, such as nice, nicer, and nicest. Some start with more and most, or less and least.

Match the adjective with the picture.

big   bigger   biggest

dangerous   more dangerous   most dangerous

LETTERS

A friendly letter normally has five parts.
You skip a line between each part.

Camp Crystal Corners
Rt. 1
Urbane, MA 11398
June 3, 2010

> **Heading...** includes the address of the sender and a date. There is a comma after the date and before the year.

Dear Mom,

> **Greeting...** is how you say hello. It always ends with a comma.

Hello from camp! Everything here is great, but I sure miss you. I made lots of friends and have fun every day.

> **Body...** is the main text. It's the part where you write what you want to say. You skip a line between paragraphs.

Every morning, I go horseback riding. I love it! Today I have swimming lessons. Tomorrow we will have fireworks! I finished all my books. Can you send some more? Thanks!

> **Close...** is a few words or one word to say goodbye. It always ends with a comma.

Love,
Emma

> **Signature...** is the part where you sign the letter.

POEMS

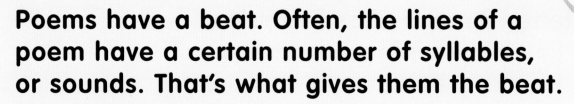

Poems have a beat. Often, the lines of a poem have a certain number of syllables, or sounds. That's what gives them the beat.

Sometimes lines rhyme, too. That means the last words sound alike.

There are two sets of rhyming words in the poem. Can you find them?

Stopping by Woods on a Snowy Evening

Whose woods these are I think I know
His house is in the village though;
He will not see me stopping here
To watch his woods fill up with snow.

My little horse must think it queer
To stop without a farmhouse near
Between the woods and frozen lake
The darkest evening of the year.
.

STORIES

A simile is a comparison using "like" or "as." A metaphor is a comparison that does not use like or as. Both are figures of speech.

Simile	Metaphor
The baby is as sweet as an angel.	The baby is an angel.

Can you say which sentence is a simile and which is a metaphor?

The toast was like a brick.

It was raining cats and dogs.

My room is a box.

The horse was as big as an elephant.

NOTES FOR PARENTS AND TEACHERS

- Children can practice spelling with unusual materials, such as shaving cream, sand, or art-and-craft materials.

- Let children create a personal dictionary of words they have difficulty spelling. Children can then refer to a dictionary as needed.

- Use self-adhesive note papers to put names on common items at home.

- Teach children words that have the same spelling pattern together, such as other, brother, and mother.

- Show children how to listen for the order of sounds in a word.

- Have children break words into syllables in order to hear smaller groups of sounds.

- Do not worry if children write letters backward. This is very common for young learners. Teach them tricks for remembering directions, but avoid scolding.

- Help children write out their spelling words with colored glue onto notecards. When the glue has dried, have them trace over the letters with their fingers while spelling the words aloud.

- Create clapping chants to accompany each spelling word. The rhythm of the chant will remind children how many letters to use and help them to remember the spellings.

SPELLING

SHORT VOWELS

Many words have a short vowel sound.
When you hear a word with a short vowel sound, it may have a CVC pattern. CVC means consonant-vowel-consonant.

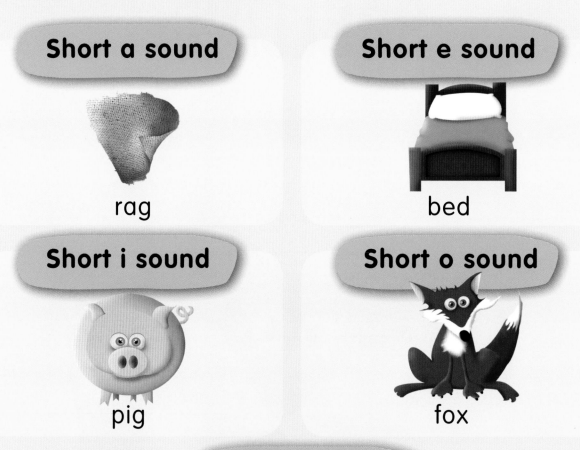

Short a sound

rag

Short e sound

bed

Short i sound

pig

Short o sound

fox

Short u sound

mud

LONG A AND E

The long a sound sounds just like the letter a. When you hear the long a sound, spell it one of these ways.

a+e sound

cake

ai sound

train

ay sound

tray

When you add an e to a CVC word, the middle vowel gets a long sound.

man ⟶ mane

For each word beginning below, point to its correct ending sound.

g_ _ _   ay
pl_ _   ake
b_ _ _   ain

27

LONG I, O, AND U

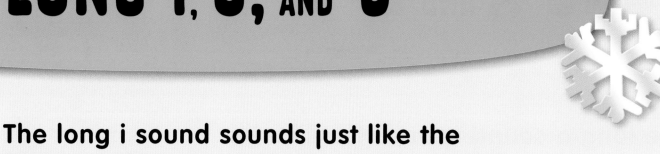

The long i sound sounds just like the letter i. When you hear the long i sound, spell it one of these ways.

CVCe sound

bike

y sound

sky

igh sound

light

When you add an e to a CVC word, the middle vowel gets a long sound.

kit ⟶ kite

The long u sound sounds just like the letter u. When you hear the long u sound, spell it like this.

CVCe sound

mule

OO AND OW SOUNDS

Vowels can work in teams to make different sounds. When you hear words with these sounds, spell them with these vowel teams.

oo sound

spoon

ow sound

cow

ou sound

mouse

Read the meanings, then point to the correct word from the word bank

If you're not sure, counting the spaces below may help.

1. A small rodent: __ __ __ __ __

2. The beginning of a question: __ __ __

3. Lights up the night: __ __ __ __

4. Another name for dog: __ __ __ __ __ __

5. Immediately: __ __ __

now
hound
moon
how
mouse

AW SOUNDS

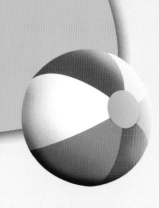

Letters can work in teams to make different sounds.
When you hear words with these sounds, spell them with these vowel teams.

aw sound

saw

all sound

ball

Do you need to add "aw" or "all" to spell the words below?

c__ __ __   m__ __ __

f__ __ __   sh__ __ l

cr__ __ l   b__ __ l

h__ __ __   b__ __ __

R-CONTROLED VOWELS

When the letter r follows a vowel, it changes the sound the vowel makes.

These are called r-controled vowels. Say the words aloud so you can hear how the vowel changes.

ar sound

car

er sound

water

ir sound

fir

or sound

porch

ur sound

turn

CLUSTERS

Consonant clusters are two or more consonants that blend together.

Each consonant make a sound, but they blend together. When you hear these sounds, spell them like this.

br sound
brown

gl sound
glee

st sound
stamp

tr sound
train

cl sound
clover

sw sound
swan

CONSONANTS AND H

When two or more consonants are next to each other and make a sound, you call this a digraph.

Some digraphs end in h. Read these words to recognize digraph sounds and spellings.

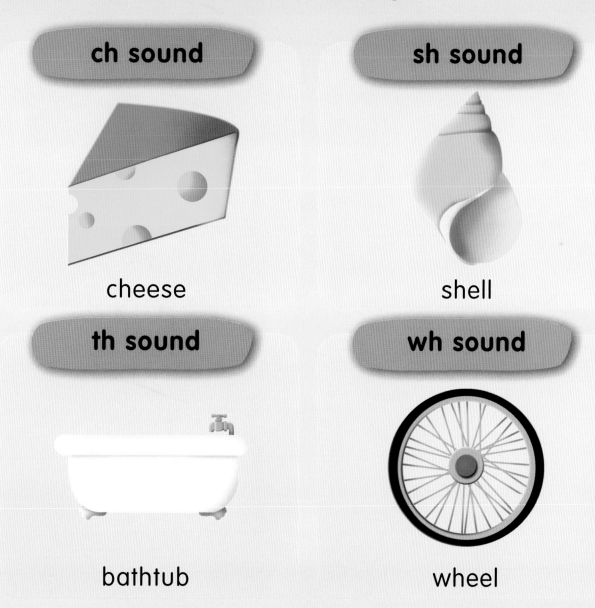

ch sound

cheese

sh sound

shell

th sound

bathtub

wh sound

wheel

HARD AND SOFT C

The letter c has two different sounds.
Hard c sounds like a k. Soft c sounds like an s.
The letter k only makes the hard c sound. If you
hear words with c sounds, spell them like this.

c sound

cake

k sound

fork

ck sound

kick

s sound

city

HARD AND SOFT G

The letter g has two different sounds. Neither sound is like another letter. If you hear words with g sounds, spell them like this.

hard g sound

goat

soft g sound

gym

Read the words below. Which words have hard g sounds and which have soft g sounds?

magic	gym	gum	age
golf	glad	gem	hug
huge	game	page	

NOTES FOR PARENTS AND TEACHERS

Here is a list of useful words and terms that are highlighted in **bold** in the following section:

capital letter	Big letter, such as A, B, or C (instead of a, b, or c).
document	Piece of typed work on the computer.
highlight	To show up br ightly; on the computer, highlighted words appear on a colored background.
paragraph	Block of writing made up of one or more sentences.
punctuation	Period, comma, dash, or other mark that helps us to read a sentence.
speech bubble	In a picture, a line drawn around the words a person is saying.
type	To press keys on the keyboard to make writing appear on the screen.
word bank	Set of words to choose from to use in your work.

STARTING WITH WORDS

ABOUT STARTING WITH WORDS

We use printed words to tell people things. Can you see printed words all around you? You'll find them on posters, books, labels, containers, comics—even on your clothes!

You can print words on a computer. Sometimes this is more useful than writing with a pen or pencil.

Ali
Rajah
2nd grade
History

Ali
Rajah
2nd grade
Math

Ali
Rajah
2nd grade
English

Ali
Rajah
2nd grade
Art

A computer helps make your work neater. You can make changes without your writing getting messy. You can print lots of copies, too.

You are invited to Jade's Party

39

You can use the keyboard to **type** words in a **document** on the computer.

Making letters

The keyboard has a key for each letter—and some other keys, which we'll look at later.

To make a letter appear on the screen, press the key with the letter that you want, then lift your finger off it again right away.

If you hold down a key, the same letter will appear again—and again, and again!

lots of kisses
XXXXXXXXX

Shift
key

Capitals

To begin a sentence, or at the start of a name, you need a **capital letter**.

To make a capital letter, hold down the Shift key and then press the letter. Let go of both keys when you see the letter appear on screen.

Practice!

Type your name, starting with a capital letter.

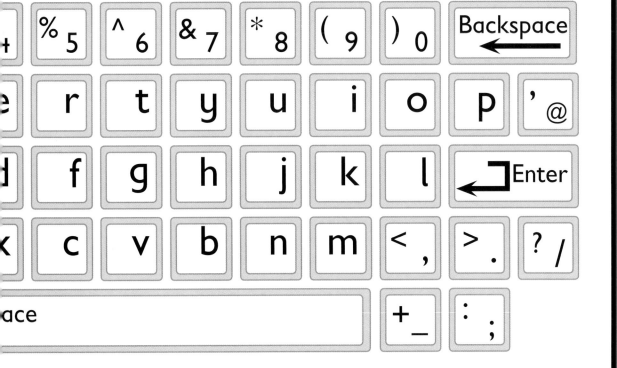

WORDS AND SENTENCES

To make whole sentences you need to add spaces between words and use end punctuation.

Space between words

At the end of a word, press the Space bar at the bottom of the keyboard. Then start the next word.

Oops!

If you make a mistake when you're typing, press the Backspace or Delete key.

This takes away the last thing you typed—just like erasing it!

Backspace or Delete key

Space bar

End punctuation

Each sentence needs a capital letter at the start and a period, exclamation point, or question mark at the end.

 Can you find the key for a period on the keyboard?

The period key looks like this: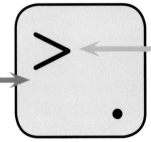

Just press the key to get a period.

If you hold down the Shift key while you press the period key, you'll get the > at the top.

Numbers

There's a key for each number —they're along the top of the keyboard.

Practice!

Try copying this sentence:
My dog is big and friendly.

NEW LINES

If you want to make a longer piece of writing, such as a story, you'll need to write more than one line.

Starting a new line

If you type a whole line of words, the computer will start a new line for you on its own—you don't need to do anything.

But if you want to start a new line before you get to the end, press the Enter key.

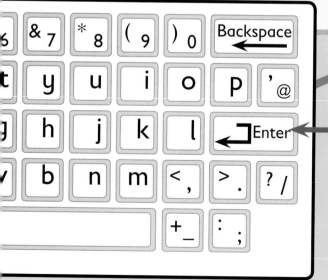

Enter key

You need to start new lines when you make a list, type an address, or make a set of labels.

We have moved.
My new address is:

Lucy Brown
4 Lilac Road
New Town
NY 11378

We have moved.
My new address is:

Practice!

Copy this list. You can change the favorites if you like.

My favorite animals are:

1. sharks
2. rabbits
3. hamsters

For my birthday I would like:

a new bike
a puzzle
a football
some books

ARRANGING WORDS

You can space your words and lines out on the page to make your work look better —or more special.

Writing poems

When you write a poem, you'll need to start lots of new lines.

You can also leave an empty line between verses.

Press Enter twice to do this.

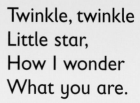

Twinkle, twinkle
Little star,
How I wonder
What you are.

Up above
The world so high,
Like a diamond
In the sky.

Twinkle, twinkle
Little star,
How I wonder
What you are.

You can use the Space bar to arrange words in your poem, too.

Humpty Dumpty sat on the wall

Humpty Dumpty had a great

F
A
L
L

Letter pictures

You can even make pictures from letters and spaces.

```
                    H        H
                    H        H
egg                 HHHH
eggegg              H        H
eggeggegg           H        H
eggeggegg
eggegg
egg
```

Practice!

Can you type the word "triangle" over and over to make a triangle?

```
        tri
       angle
     triangletri
    angletriangletri
   angletriangletriangle
  triangletriangletriangletri
```

WORD BANKS

It can take a long time to type your words when you start using the computer. At school, your computer probably has a **word bank** so you can pick a word without having to type it.

Hello

What is a word bank?

A word bank is a list of words on the screen. This is a special list of words your teacher has made for you to use to do your work.

Some word banks speak the words to you, so you can choose words even if you can't read them.

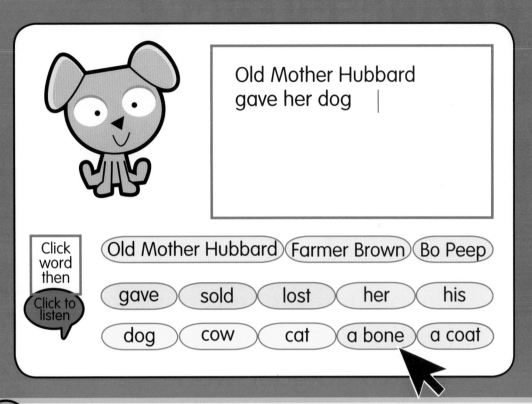

Old Mother Hubbard
gave her dog

Click word then
Click to listen

Old Mother Hubbard | Farmer Brown | Bo Peep
gave | sold | lost | her | his
dog | cow | cat | a bone | a coat

Choosing a word

You need to click on the word, and then on a button, to listen to the word or copy it into your work. It's a good idea to listen to all the words so you pick the best one.

For lunch today I ate ....

pizza | salad | pasta | apple

banana | cheese | chicken | tomato

click to choose

MAKING CHANGES

Sometimes you need to make changes to your work.

Maybe you made a mistake, or thought of a better way to do your work.

Adding words

You can add more words anywhere you want in your document.

Just click where you want to make a change and start typing. The new words will appear in between the words you've already typed.

The Three Frogs

click and type

The Three Pink Dotted Frogs

Adding space

To add a space between words, click where you want the space, and then press the Space bar.

twowords

two words

click here and press Space bar

You can split up a line, too, or add more blank lines. Click where you want to split or add a line and press Enter.

Spelling book Carl

click here and press Enter

Spelling book
Carl

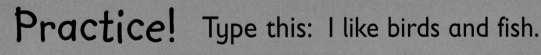

Practice! Type this: I like birds and fish.

and change it to this: I like blue birds and green fish.

51

A BIT DIFFERENT

Sometimes you want to make a few documents that are slightly different. It's easy to change what you've typed—and you don't need to type it all over again.

Changing words

Sometimes you want to replace one word with another.

Dear Sarah,

Please come to my party on Saturday at 3 p.m.

Love, Jessica

Sarah

click and hold

1. Put the mouse pointer before the first letter.

Erase the words

If you want to get rid of some words completely, you can do it like this.

| I ~~don't~~ like soccer. | I like soccer. |

1. Highlight the word, just as if you were going to change it.

2. Press the Delete or Backspace key to erase the word.

| Sar|ah | Sarah| | Lily| |

2. Press the mouse button and move the mouse along to **highlight** the word.

3. Take your finger off the mouse button when the word is highlighted.

4. Type in your new word.

Dear Lily,

Please come to my party on Saturday at 3 p.m.

Love, Jessica

BIG AND SMALL

If you look around you, you'll see that words are printed in different sizes.

LOST CAT

Ziggy

A white cat with a gray patch on his head.
Please call (213) 555-3890

Big and bold

If something has to be read from far away, or it's important that people notice it, it's usually printed in large letters.

STOP!

The words in books for young children are usually printed in large sizes with only a few words on each page. Books for adults have lots of words that are in smaller print.

cat
dog
ball
kite

Volcanoes

Volcanoes are mountains that spurt fire and hot rock into the air.
They can be very dangerous. The hot rock from a volcano comes from far underground. The Earth has a layer of molten hot rock over 1,800 miles thick.

In newspapers, headlines are bigger than the rest of the words so you notice them first.

Daily News • 20 July 2005

Grrreat escape!

A dangerous Bengal tiger escaped yesterday afternoon from a zoo in San Diego.

Dinosaurs
2nd Grade Project

Some of the biggest dinosaurs ate plants.

Some ancient reptiles could even fly. They were bigger than birds.

Your work

Your teacher will help you set the size of words when you use the computer at school.

You would use bigger letters for a poster or wall chart than for your name labels.

Joe Young

Joe

GET IT RIGHT

Always check your work when you're done. Make sure you haven't made any mistakes.

Read through your work

- Are the words spelled correctly?
- Have you left spaces between the words?
- Have you used **punctuation** and capital letters?
- Is there enough space between the **paragraphs**?
- If you find any mistakes, correct them.

my freind iscalled alice

My friend is called Alice.

Even better

Can you think of ways to make your work better?

Try a more interesting word, such as a "huge" cake instead of a "big" cake, or a boy who "jumped" out of bed instead of "got" out of bed.

Make any changes and then check your work again.

a **big** cake

a **huge** cake

Toby **got** out of bed.

Toby **jumped** out of bed.

Get help

Ask someone else to read your work. They can look for mistakes you missed or think of ways to make it better.

PRINT YOUR WORK

It's nice to do your work on the computer—but even better if you can print it out to show to other people or take home!

Getting ready to print

Before you print your work, check it carefully so that you don't waste paper printing it with lots of mistakes.

What color?

You can print your work on colored paper if you like. It's a good way to make it stand out.

Printing

There is a print button on the screen. Click on it to print your work on paper.

Another look

Read through your work after you have printed it. If you find any more mistakes, correct them and print it out again!

59

OVER TO YOU

On the next four pages, find out how to type and print your own story!

Think of a story…

Think of a story you'd like to write. It can be a story you've made up, or a fairy tale, or another story you've heard or read.

Draw pictures for the story on four sheets of paper.

?

Are there people talking? If so, you could draw empty **speech bubbles** on your pictures.

Type the words

Now type out the words for your story on the computer.

Leave a blank line after each sentence.

Jess found an egg on the ground.

She made a nest and a bird to watch over it.

She kept the egg warm.

She waited for it to hatch.

The egg started to crack.

Now type the words for the speech bubbles.

Do not write too much, or your words will not fit into the bubbles you have drawn.

Come on, you can do it.

Snap

Cut and glue

Check your work, make any changes, and then print it out.

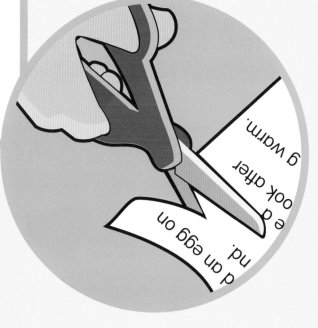

Cut up the page so each sentence is on a separate strip of paper.

Glue the words in the right places on your story pages.

Now print out the "talking words." Cut them up and stick them inside the speech bubbles in the right places.

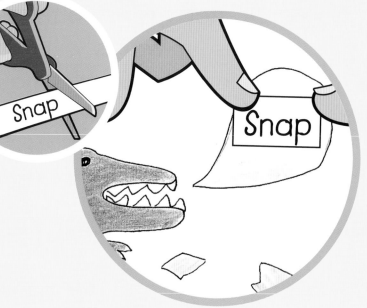

Jess found an egg on the ground.

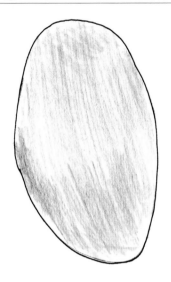

1

She made a nest and a bird to watch over it.

She kept the egg warm. 2

She waited for it to hatch.

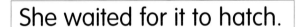

The egg started to crack. 3

Hooray!

It was a baby crocodile! 4

NOTES FOR PARENTS AND TEACHERS

Here is a list of useful words and terms that are highlighted in **bold** in the following section:

contents List of main topics covered in a book or CD-ROM.

icon Small picture that stands for something.

index List of subject words that appear in a book or CD-ROM.

information Facts about something.

keyword Word you use to carry out a search on a CD-ROM.

link One or more words or objects that if you click on them, will open a new page on a CD-ROM or website.

menu List of things you can choose from on the computer.

multimedia Information on the computer that uses a mixture of words, pictures, sounds, and video footage.

search Tool used to find out about a topic.

talking book Storybook on the computer that will read words out to you.

FINDING FACTS

ABOUT FINDING FACTS

You see and hear all kinds of **information** every day. Some of it you find for yourself—you read a book, ask a question, or watch TV. But lots of it is just around you, trying to make you notice it!

Observing information

What information can you see around you right now? To start, there's this book! But you can probably see posters, wall displays, labels, and writing.

Pictures, such as signs, maps, paintings, and cartoons, give us information.

Words people say give information, too. We talk to each other and listen to CDs, the radio, and the television.

On the computer

A computer shows you information in words, pictures, and sounds.

Other sounds give information— the school bell, a fire alarm, and a police siren all tell us something.

WHAT DOES IT MEAN?

Information has all sorts of messages. It can warn us, teach us, or make us laugh.

Time to get up!

What's it telling you?

Some information tells you useful things—like the way out of the supermarket, or which restroom is for boys and which for girls, how to play a game, or when it's safe to cross the road.

PLEASE DO NOT FEED

How do we know?

If you see a sign showing a bicycle crossed out, you can guess it means "No Biking." That is because you can "read" the message in the picture.

Advertisements try to get you to spend money.

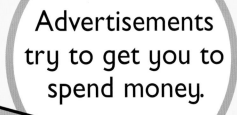

STORING INFORMATION

You can use the computer to store your work—and all kinds of other information, too.

Doing it yourself

When you do your own work on the computer, you use the keyboard and the mouse to put in the words you want. You can use the mouse to draw pictures if you have a painting or drawing program.

When you've finished your work, you can print it out so you have a copy on paper that you can show to other people.

You can also save your work onto a CD-ROM so you can use it again later.

Making choices

Sometimes the computer needs to ask you a question. It appears on the screen. You can type your answer or choose one by clicking on a button.

Do you want to save your work?

click to choose

Menus

The computer can offer you choices by showing you a set of words or pictures called a **menu**.

Choose a picture to color in

click to choose

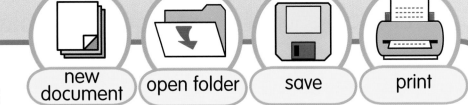

new document | open folder | save | print

Pictures

The computer uses **icons**—little pictures that stand for something. You've probably seen some of these icons and may already know what they mean.

LISTEN CAREFULLY!

Sometimes the computer speaks words. This is helpful if you can't read all the words on the screen.

All ears

Sounds can give you extra information, such as playing a tune or teaching you animal noises. That's something most books can't do!

The computer can play sound as soon as you open the screen, or there will be a button to click on to hear sound.

Farmyard sounds

Mooo

click to choose

Sounds for fun

Games often use sounds, such as the sound of cars in a racing game. Sounds can make the game much more exciting.

Screech

Brmm, brmm

When computers use sounds, pictures, words, and even moving cartoons or video film, it's called **multimedia**. You can use multimedia for fun or to find things out.

All about frogs

See frog photos

Hear frog sounds

Watch frog videos

Frogs lay eggs which are called frogspawn—when they hatch, they are called tadpoles.

TELLING STORIES

You can read or listen to stories from books, or use the computer.

Talking books

A talking book on the computer tells a story using words, pictures, and sounds. You can read the story yourself on the screen, or get the computer to read it to you.

This is the story of Waltrude the witch and Fin her cat...

click to hear the story

74

Practice!

If you've got a talking book, try this:

Find a button to click to make the computer read the words.

Move the mouse over a word.

She cast a spell.

Abracadabra

click to hear the word

If the computer doesn't read it out, click on the word. Does it read now?

Coming to life

You can click buttons or move across parts of the picture to play sounds or see moving pictures.

Meow

click to play

WHAT HAPPENS NEXT?

In a paper book, you turn the pages to move on to the next part of the story or check back to see what happened before. With a talking book, you move to a new page using the mouse.

Follow the arrow

A talking book usually has arrow buttons on the screen for you to go forward or backward.

Click the arrow pointing to the right to move on to the next page.
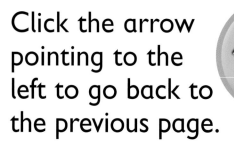

Click the arrow pointing to the left to go back to the previous page.

Click on double arrows to go all the way back to the beginning:  or all the way to the end of the book:

You choose!

In a storybook, you have to read from the beginning to the end, otherwise it doesn't make sense.

Some talking books are like this, but others let you make choices.

What happens next in the story depends on what you choose.

This way   That way

click to choose

Practice!

Try moving forward and backward through a talking book. Read the whole story.

FINDING THINGS OUT

There are lots of ways to find out things you want to know.

Using books

You can get some information from a person or from a book.

You could ask your teacher how big a tiger is, or you could look in a book about tigers.

Or you could watch TV programs or DVDs about tigers.

If you want to find out a fact, it's usually quicker to ask or look in a book. You could watch a whole DVD and not find what you wanted.

Are we there yet?

Many books give you help to find what you want. They have a **contents** page or an **index** so you can look up what you want to know.

Ask a friend

For some kinds of information, the way to find out something is to ask someone. You ask the cafeteria cook what's for lunch, or you ask a friend what day their birthday is on.

IT'S ALL LINKED

You can look things up on the computer, too.

Links

CD-ROMs usually have an index and a contents list, just like a book. But they also have something books don't have—they have **links** between the pages so you can jump around.

If a word is linked to another page, it usually has a line under it. It might also be in a different color.

Just click on the linked word to make the new page come up on the screen.

Animals of the World

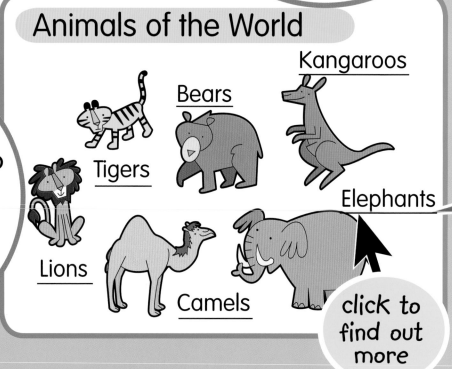

Kangaroos

Bears

Tigers

Lions

Camels

Elephants

click to find out more

More information

It can be much faster to look up information on a computer than in a book. If a book says "elephants (see page 10)," you have to turn to that page for the information you need.

On the computer, the word "elephants" is linked to the other page. Just click on it to see all about elephants.

Elephants

Elephants come from India and Africa.

Practice!

If you've got a CD-ROM, follow five links and see where you get to. Can you get back to where you started?

MOVING AROUND

If you follow lots of links, you might get lost! Luckily, books on CD-ROM have buttons to help you find your way around.

Going back

When you follow a link, you can easily get back to where you were before. Look for an arrow with the word "Back" pointing to the left. This will take you back to the last page you looked at.

Back

You might be on a page about rockets. Then you click on a link to astronauts. To get back to rockets again, just click the Back button.

Rockets
Rockets take astronauts into <u>space</u>.
Fire comes out of the engine at the back of the rocket as it takes off.

go back to the last page that you looked at

Back

Astronauts
An astronaut wears a special suit and an air tank to work in space.

go back one page

go back to the beginning

go to the end

go forward one page

Remember that there are other arrows on the page, too. They take you forward or back one page, or right to the beginning or end of the topic.

MORE MOVING

You won't always want to move through the CD-ROM in order. You can move around in other ways, too.

Going home

Sometimes, there's a button to go right back to the beginning. It often has a picture of a house because the first page is called the "home" page.

Contents

Index

What else is there?

There is usually a button to go to the index or contents page, or for both.

The index or contents list of a CD-ROM doesn't have page numbers, like in a book. Instead, it has links.

The contents shows a list of what's on the CD-ROM.

CONTENTS

Look after your pet:

 Cat

 Dog

 Fish

 Rabbit

 Rabbits

A rabbit needs a hutch and somewhere to run around. It needs clean water and fresh food each day.

click to find out more

The index lists lots of words you may want to look for on the CD-ROM, to help you find a topic.

INDEX

cat	kitten
dog	leash
fish food	puppy
rabbit food	rabbit
hay	tank
hutch	weed

click to find topic

KEEP SEARCHING

If you can't find what you want in the index or contents, you can ask the computer to look for it.

Find or search

Many CD-ROMs have a **Search** button. This lets you look for one or more words.

Click the Search button to see a box where you can type in the word you want to look for.

Search

Type word here

click here to search

Using keywords

The word you search for is called a "**keyword**." Choosing the right keyword takes a little practice.

Imagine you have a CD-ROM about animals and you want to find out about baby cats. If you can't find a link from the cats page, you could search for "baby."

baby

But the computer doesn't know you want to find out about baby cats and will suggest other baby animals, and cats, too.

Searching for "kitten" or "baby cat" will take you right to what you need.

kitten

OVER TO YOU

Now it's time to do some work of your own. You'll need a CD-ROM that has a contents list or index, and links between the pages.

Treasure hunt!

Make a treasure hunt for words. Then ask a friend to find the treasure.

1. Choose a linked word from the contents list. Write it down on paper.

2. Click on the link to open the linked page.

3. On the page that opens, pick another link.

4. Again, write down a linked word, then click on it.

5. Do this until you've followed at least three links.

6. Write a clue for your friend, to help them click on the first word you wrote down.

For example, if you chose "turtles," your clue could be:

It's green or brown, and hides in its hard shell.

Make sure only one topic on the page fits your clue.

Turtles

Some turtles live on the land, and some in the <u>water</u>.

Water

Most of the Earth is covered in water. We find it in the <u>oceans</u>, in <u>rivers,</u> and even in <u>clouds</u>.

Rivers

In some places, rivers are more important than <u>roads</u>. They are used for <u>transportation</u>.

7. Think of a clue for each of your other links, right through to the final answer.

8. Tell your friend to open the contents page of the CD-ROM. Give them the clues and see how they do!

MAKE A TALKING BOOK

Make your own **talking book** —without using the computer!

You'll need six pieces of paper.

1. Draw six pictures to make a story or copy the pictures on the next page. Write a line of words above each picture.

2. On each page, draw arrows to go forward and backward, back to the beginning, and right to the end.

3. Decide what will happen on each page. Then draw a star where someone could click to see or hear something.

Imagine, if your talking book was on the computer, what could it do? If someone clicked on an animal or person, would it make a noise? Or would it do an action?

1. Frank the cat fell asleep in the garden.

2. A bird flew by.

3. The bird landed near Frank.

4. Frank pounced on the bird.

5. The bird pecked Frank on the head.

6. Lucy put a bandaid on Frank.

Peck, peck

4. Ask a friend to use your book—you have to pretend to be the computer!

If your friend points at an arrow, give them the right page.

If they point at a sentence, read it out.

If they point at a star, do the action or sound!

NOTES FOR PARENTS AND TEACHERS

Here is a list of useful words and terms that are highlighted in **bold** in the following section:

classify Arranging things in a certain way, such as into groups.

icon A small picture that stands for something.

information Facts about something.

investigate Finding out as much as possible about something.

pictogram A picture that stands for a word or meaning.

record To write facts down or take note of them. Keeping a record can help you remember facts.

sorting To arrange facts in a way that makes sense, such as into groups.

survey Asking lots of people the same questions and taking recording their answers.

vote Making a decision on something in a survey. For example, you can vote for your favorite color.

MAKING
CHARTS

ABOUT MAKING CHARTS

You can often find out as much from pictures as from reading words. Some **information** is easier to understand in a picture.

Some facts can be shown clearly in a picture or chart.

Imagine you've collected a variety of sea creatures from the beach:

You could put them in groups to help you see what you've found.

This is called **sorting** or **classifying** objects.

Then you can count each group and make a chart like this one.

The chart is divided into columns, or bars. The size of the columns shows how many you found of each.

Which is the tallest column? This shows that you found mostly scallops.

These pages show you how to make and understand charts like this. They are called **pictograms**.

FINDING OUT

To make your own pictogram, you need to find out some information. There are lots of ways to do this. You can ask people, or count things, or measure them.

Information from other people

Sometimes you get your information from other people. You can ask them questions or ask them to **vote** for a favorite of some kind.

What's your favorite ice-cream flavor?

Information from things

Lots of information comes from counting things.

You could count how many people in your class have dark hair, how many have blonde hair, and how many have red hair.

Color of hair in our class
Brown hair ///////
Red hair //
Blonde hair /////
Black hair ///

Weather at lunchtime
Monday = sunny
Tuesday = rainy
Wednesday = sunny
Thursday = cloudy
Friday = cloudy

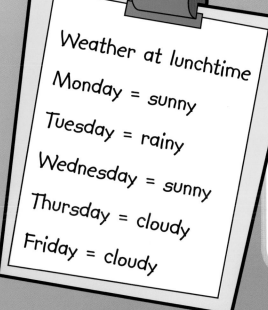

You can record the weather at lunchtime for a week and list the days it rained, the days it was cloudy, and the days it was sunny.

ASKING QUESTIONS

When you make a chart, you can get your information from other people.

You can ask people to put their hand up if a dog is their favorite pet, or a cat, and so on. You just need to count the hands each time.

Making a survey

You could also do a **survey**. This is useful if the people you want to ask aren't in the same place at the same time. You write down your questions and ask people, one at a time, to give their answers.

98

Decide the best way to ask your question.

If you just ask people which animal is the scariest, you could get too many different answers to make a pictogram.

Which animal are you most scared of?

tiger /// crab,

lion, wolf

scorpion, bee //

hippo

fierce dog

shark //   snake

wasp

slug

X

It's best to give people answers to choose from. Then you know all the answers will fit your pictogram.

Which of these is the scariest animal?

shark ////
tiger //
lion ///
spider ////
wasp /

✓

sharks

INVESTIGATE

Another way to **investigate** is to do an experiment and **record** the results, or take measurements.

Fruit
apples ////////
bananas //
grapes /////
pears ///
oranges //

Try looking at the type of fruit in everyone's lunchbox and write down which fruit people have brought to school.

Less is more!

Don't try to get too much information. A small number of choices is easier to record.

If you take measurements, make sure you always measure things in the same way so you make a fair comparison.

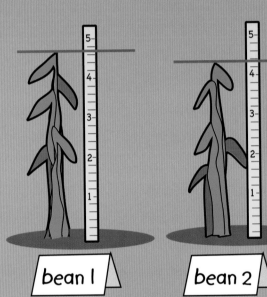

bean 1

bean 2

When you record a measurement, use the nearest whole number.

height of beans week 6

bean 1 = 5 in

bean 2 = 4 in

Enough!

Small numbers of things will also make your chart easier for others to read.

CHECK IT!

It's a good idea to check that you are getting your information in the best way. Some ways are better than others!

At the gate

Suppose you wanted to find out how children come to school. One way is to stand at the gate counting people as they arrive.

How children get to school

car / / / / / / / / / / / / / /

bus / / / / / / / / / / / /

biking / / / / / / / / / / /

walking / / / / / / / / / / /

The hard way

It's hard to count the number of children in cars and buses, because lots of children arrive at the same time.

A better way

You could go to every class and ask how many people come to school by each form of transportation.

Mr. Bell's class
30 children
car //////////
bus //////////
biking /////
walking /////

Final check

• Count the number of people in the survey and the total tally. Are they the same?
• Did you measure or count the right things?
• Did you ask the right questions?

LINES AND PILES

A pictogram shows a picture of each thing in a column or bar. It's not the same as making a line or a pile in real life.

Make a line

Ask everyone to bring their coats in from the cloakroom. Sort the coats by color and put them in separate lines—red coats, blue ones, white ones, etc.

Count how many coats there are in each line. Some coats are bigger than others, so the most common coat color probably won't make the longest line.

Pile them up

Now make piles of coats. Put each line of colored coats into a separate pile.

Your piles aren't like a pictogram. You can't tell from the height of the piles which is the most common color.

Some coats might not fit your piles easily, and you will need to start a new pile.

Neat and tidy

A pictogram would use the same size of picture for each coat. You could tell how many there are of each color from the heights of the columns.

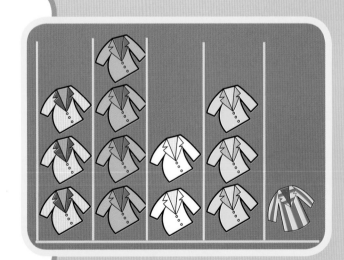

LOOKING GOOD

To help people understand your chart, it should be easy to read, and the pictures you use need to match your information.

Using icons

Your teacher will help you pick pictures that show what your chart is about. Pictures used like this are called **icons**.

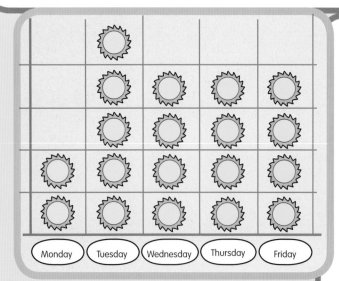

You can use the same icon in each column. If you counted the hours of sunshine each day for a week, you could use suns in each column.

The icons could also be completely different. If your chart shows the fruit people have in their lunchboxes, you can use a different fruit picture in each column.

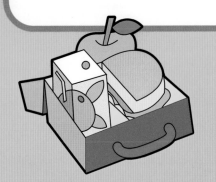

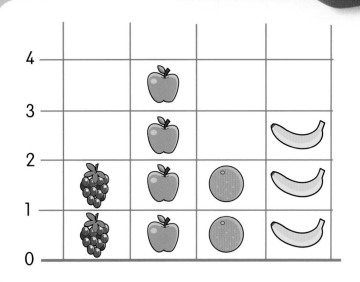

How many icons?

Look at the information you have gathered for your chart. Does it need just one icon or lots of different icons? If it needs lots, which ones?

START A CHART

It's time to practice putting information into a chart on the computer.

Getting started

You will be able to choose how many columns to have on your pictogram.

You can also give a name, or label, to each column.

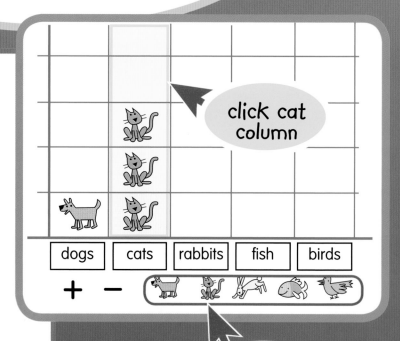

click cat column

dogs | cats | rabbits | fish | birds

then click cat four times to enter 4 cats

Type the numbers or click a button for each number. If you wanted to enter "4" for the cats column, click on the cat picture four times.

Get it right!

If you make a mistake, correct it. When you're finished, check the numbers again by looking at the information you found out.

- Have you copied all the numbers correctly?

- Have you missed any numbers?

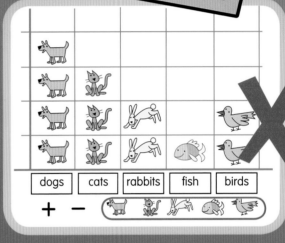

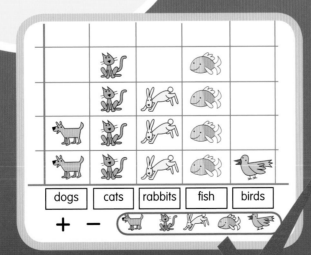

MAKING SENSE

You know what the chart is about—but other people need to be able to read it, too.

Use a title

You need a title that explains what the chart shows. Make it short, but clear.

Fruit in lunches

How we get to school

How many in my family

Favorite fish

Numbers

Putting numbers up the side of the chart helps people see how many things there are in each column without having to count them.

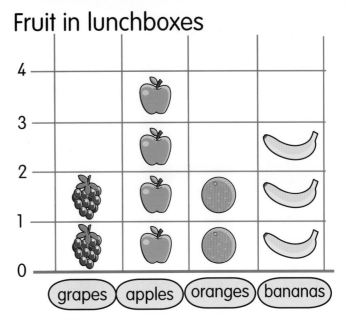

Fruit in lunchboxes

grapes   apples   oranges   bananas

Anything else?

You can put the date on your chart if it will help people understand it. If it is a weather chart, it matters whether it was in summer or winter. Four snowy days in a row would be more surprising in the summer than in the winter!

WHAT DOES IT MEAN?

Looking at a pictogram can tell you a lot of information.

How many?

You can see from the height of each column how many things are in each group.

You can see how many children have each color in their bedroom. How many people have pink bedrooms?

The color of our bedrooms

	green	blue	pink	white	purple

Picking favorites

Compare the size of the columns. The tallest one shows you which is the most common color.

The most common color of bedroom is blue. Pink and green are the second most common colors.

The least common colour is purple— only one person has a purple bedroom.

Comparing

The column for blue bedrooms is twice as tall as the column for white bedrooms. This tells you that twice as many people have blue bedrooms as white bedrooms.

WHAT DOESN'T IT MEAN?

It's good to know what a chart shows you, but it's important to remember there are some things it doesn't show you.

Be careful!

In the chart, more people have blue bedrooms than any other color, but that doesn't mean most people have blue bedrooms.

Of the 13 bedrooms in the chart only four are blue—that's less than half!

You can't say that blue is the children's favorite color for bedrooms.

Perhaps the children weren't allowed to choose the color. Or they might share a bedroom with a brother or sister and had to agree on a color they both liked.

You can't tell...

You can't tell from the chart which child has which color.

You can't tell whether more girls than boys have pink bedrooms.

You can't tell whether older children all have blue bedrooms.

You can't tell if shared bedrooms are more likely to be painted white.

OVER TO YOU

Now it's time to make a pictogram of your own.

Which sport do you like best?

What pets do you have?

Choosing a subject

Decide what your pictogram will show. Here are some ideas, but you could choose something totally different:

- What kinds of pets people have.

- Favorite sports.

- Types of trees—in your backyard, at school, or in the park.

Getting information

Work out exactly what information you need. Remember to ask your question in the same way every time. Make sure people understand the question and the type of answer you need.

Don't choose a subject that will be too difficult to investigate.

- If you are counting things or people, make sure your numbers are right.

- If you look at how people come to school, are you going to count people or types of transportation?

- If you look at fruit in lunchboxes, don't count each grape separately!

Making your chart

Put your information into the computer. Check that you've spelled everything correctly, and fix any mistakes. Choose icons that show what your pictogram is about, and add labels.

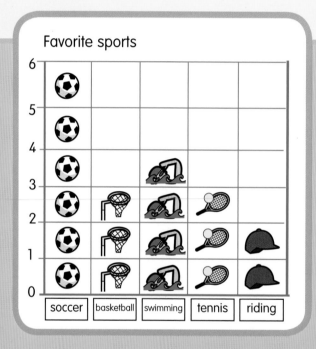

Favorite sports

What have you found out?

What can you tell from your chart? Which is the best-liked sport? Do children prefer apples or oranges for lunch?

What don't you know?

What sort of information can't you tell from your chart? Is the information you've got the most useful? Or do people want to know different facts?

Check your work

Think about how you've made your chart.

• Would different icons have been better?

• Could you have used clearer labels?

• Did you ask enough people?

• Can you make the chart any better?

OTHER TITLES IN THIS SERIES

Fun with Phonics
Find out what the monsters are doing
today and have some fun with phonics!

Fun with Math
Discover exciting activities, with the help of some
colorful characters, and have some fun with math!

Fun with Drawing and Painting
Find out about all the different ways you can draw
and paint and have some fun with art!

Fun with Prints and Special Effects
Find out how to make the most of your
prints and have some fun with art!

GREYSCALE

BIN TRAVELER FORM

Cut By _Michael A Huerto_ Qty _10_ Date _2-19_

Scanned By_____ Qty_____ Date_____

Scanned Batch IDs

_____   _____   _____

Notes / Exception

_____

_____

_____

_____

_____